CHEERS LIFE!

D0915838

To Elizabeth's favourite Professor With best wishes Grace 6 Aug 2006

by Grace Segran

Published by Grace Segran

First published 2000

Printed in Singapore by National Photo Engravers

For information, please write to: c/o 6 Jalan Saudara-ku, Singapore 457443
or email: cheers_to_life@hotmail.com

ISBN 981-04-2880-4

Designed, edited and typeset by Dorothy Lim, PublishWrite Consultancy
Cover concept and design by Dorothy Lim

To Him Who is Able
Be all Glory, Honour and Praise

For my two Best Friends,
Raja and Bessie
I love you guys

CONTENTS

Bare facts, statistics and exhortations. Doctors are good at dispensing these. They roll off our tongues smoothly, falling heavily upon our patients' ears, impressing upon them the potency of this disease.

The litany of words marches on – "breast cancer, the commonest cancer among women worldwide; nearly 900,000 new cases each year and the leading cancer-killer of over 300,000 women annually. In Singapore, more than 1000 women are afflicted every year and the numbers are expected to rise with an ageing population. Women need to be vigilant about breast self-examination. Regular screening, mammography and early detection are your best defenses."

Vicariously, the gravity of the problem elevates the status of the practitioners and the would-be healers.

But after all is said and done, medical science remains remotely far from being able to assure anyone that cancer can be kept at bay or that doctors can cure the afflicted. We can't promise that plans won't be altered, or dreams always fulfilled, suffering forestalled and good books finished.

Which is why Grace's recount of her up close struggle with breast cancer is such a refreshing read. No candy-coated feel-good aphorisms or naïve clichés here. Her story shoots straight to the heart. Grace has accepted that life can be unfair and often is. Her suffering was not lessened by any intimate knowledge gained during her nursing career.

Like a fragile raft shooting the rapids, she triumphs and stays afloat despite all the attempts by this disease to rob her of her dignity and *joie de vivre*. When chemotherapy renders food tasteless, what does Grace do? Ask the cook to add more chili padi of course!

Grace's sentient experiences resonate with the truth that recovery begins with self and that cancer can do only as much as you allow it. The day will come when we finally discover a way to prevent millions of women from developing breast cancer and it will be a day of great rejoicing when we are finally rid of this dread disease. Until then, personal victories at the battlefront such as this one reminds us all that the war will have to be won a day at a time – with courage, humor and grace.

Dr Ng Eng Hen
Chairman, Medical Advisory Committee
Breast Cancer Foundation

Good friends were buying me a farewell dinner in an Italian restaurant in Clark Quay when the handphone rang. Grace, who was then in Jakarta with Bessie, was on the other end. She'd found a lump on her breast, and the doctors in Jakarta had not ruled out cancer. We agreed that she should come down to Singapore the very next day and have the doctors look at it.

Thus began a new chapter in our lives. We were in the midst of preparing for one (my posting to Jakarta) but were presented with another, different, unexpected, chapter. A nine-month interregnum that seemed, sometimes, to flash by in the twinkling of an eye, but at other times, drag on interminably, as though time stood still.

This new chapter was full of discovery, pain, growth, successes, defeats, but mostly it was a chapter about life, with every reason for its celebration.

We discovered a great deal about ourselves, drew on reserves we never thought we had. We gave in to bouts of depression that we thought we could never sink into. We learned that it was no shame to acknowledge both our weaknesses and our strengths. Most of all we discovered ourselves as people, growing as individuals, as a couple, and as a family.

We rediscovered the great support and love of friends and family. I suppose we always had them, knew them, enjoyed them, and loved them. But this crisis helped us recognize them, appreciate them, and led us to no longer take them for granted. There is no greater joy than to realise that we are not alone, that we are loved, and that people would go to unimaginable lengths to express their love to us.

But most of all this experience with cancer helped us to discover afresh the unfathomable love and unfailing faithfulness of God. We discovered with a new freshness that we are loved, blessed and watched over, by the greatest Friend of all.

I had encouraged Grace to keep a journal as we went through this chapter of our lives. It would,

I thought, be therapeutic. But more than that,
I believe nothing happens to us without purpose,
and felt that her experience could perhaps help
someone else writing the same chapter.

These pages are the result of her recollections.
May they help cancer patients and their loved
ones discover, as we did, that cancer is a word,
not a sentence. That even in the grip of this
disease we can live life, and live it abundantly.

L'chaim!
(*To life!*)

Raja Segran

ACKNOWLEDGEMENTS

Countless people have helped my family and I when I was undergoing treatment for cancer. Countless others helped to put this book together and to launch it. To name them all would take another book. So please forgive me if I can't list everyone. But there are some who must be mentioned:

My brother-in-law and his family – Guna, Christina, Simon, Thea and Reuben – who ministered to us both spiritually and physically, and in the process helped create a family tradition of dinners (and durians).

The Nicholsons and Vijay and Rathi Alfreds for lovingly looking after Bessie in Jakarta.

My doctors who have now become our friends: Dr Ang Peng Tiam and Dr Wong Sen Chow and their fabulous staff for looking after me.

Colleagues (and their families) from Singapore Airlines and SATS who encouraged us.

Friends at Changi Baptist Church and Agape Baptist Church (Singapore), and All Saints' (South Jakarta); ol' Trinitarians; and friends in Singapore and all over the world – you know who you are – who prayed, called, emailed, snail-mailed, and visited.

My family – Raja and Bessie – for your unfailing support. You encouraged me even though you were bearing the burden of my illness. My victory is yours too.

Special thanks go to the following for making this book and its launch possible:
- *My editor and friend, Dorothy Lim*
- *Mrs Jennifer Yeo for being Guest-of-Honour at the launch of this book*
- *Elizabeth Prakasam*
- *Alice Chee*
- *Kevin, Joe and Helen Lam, and her 'kakis'*
- *S. Supramaniam*
- *Richard Gomez*
- *Mrs Theresa Seah*
- *National Library Board*
- *NTUC Unity Healthcare*
- *Atmedica.com and Health Today*
- *SingTel Mobile Pte Ltd*
- *YTC Hotels Singapore*

OUR MIDNIGHT SONG

My mother and I,
We are
The same
Tiger spirit,
Raven voice.

That umbilical cord
Where spirit flowed into me
Now transmits pain
Too profound to express.

As I stand helplessly watching
Hair fall
Faces cringe
Groans bellow,
My soul shreds.

No tears puissant enough
To bear a million whirlwinds
Or the sweltering heat that
Dries the soul.

So we do not cry.

I am not alone
Pacing in the moonlight
Singing my midnight song.

Bessie Segran

THE DANCE

On 21 September, 1998, I was tapped on the shoulder and called into a dance. A dance with breast cancer. I was unprepared. But compelled.

I had to adapt my footwork to the dance. Move to its rhythm. Feel it deep in my soul.

Like the tango, it can be intense. There are fleeting moments of exhilaration and moments of repose. The partners can be oppressively close. Or one could twirl away from the other, grip slackening, until their fingers barely touch.

The pace changes. I lose myself in the swirl as everything becomes a blur. But the Choreographer knows every move in this dance. Unseen, invisible, He leads, enabling me to make brilliant moves I had never thought possible.

A dance is very personal. No one else knows what it feels like except the dancer. The dancer and the dance cannot be separated – until the music stops and the dance is over. When the dance is over, it ceases to exist, leaving the dancer the richer for the experience.

So, do not be afraid to dance. Let the music engulf you and dance with gusto.

Grace Segran

To say the nine months between September 1998 and June 1999 were exciting, would be an understatement. It was "very happening", as some Singaporeans might say.

Our lives were drastically rearranged, our plans and dreams put on hold while I underwent eight gruelling cycles of chemotherapy and 31 daily doses of radiation for Stage Two breast cancer that involved six lymph nodes.

My husband, Raja, had been posted to Jakarta. I had gone ahead a month earlier in September so that our 15 year-old daughter could start school. Ten days later I found the lump, returned to Singapore, had surgery and commenced treatment immediately.

Raja's posting was deferred so I could receive treatment in Singapore. Bessie remained in Jakarta, staying with friends, to continue her studies at the British school as she was preparing for the IGCSE 'O' levels.

For a 15-year-old teenager, an only child, to be separated from her parents under such traumatic circumstances was devastating. The separation was as painful as the diagnosis itself.

In Singapore, Raja and I tried to set up home with some semblance of normalcy. Our apartment looked like a warehouse with some 80 boxes that the movers had packed for the move that didn't take place.

We opened some boxes to retrieve things we needed for the short period that we expected to be there. What we couldn't find, we bought again. We filled the kitchen cabinets and wardrobes but the walls and shelves remained empty. The house didn't feel like home, it was so bare and cold. Cancer and everything it tainted made it even colder as it hung over our lives like a dark cloud. Gone was the bright happy home that it once was. Thankfully, it was only for a season.

We lived those nine months in transition – awaiting the completion of cancer treatment, the birth of new life, and the go-ahead to resume our posting.

It was as though the world had stopped while we went through the ordeal of chemo, radiation, separation and soul-searching. Through these times we discovered the iron in our souls we never knew we had. And we discovered the medicine called laughter.

Our lives are forever changed. We learnt to value the best things in life – faith, hope, love, friend-ships, humour. We learnt to celebrate life – both on the mountain and in the valley.

I dedicate this collection of our laughter and tears in this dance with cancer – to you.

Brae Segran

y hair started to fall off precisely two
weeks after I started chemotherapy.
Just like my oncologist had told me.
When it started coming out by the handful, I
decided to take control and shave it all off.

I had a few options on how to do it. I could go to
my hairdresser, Helen, and make an appointment
for a time after the last customer had left. She
could pull the shades down so that we would not
have the entire population of Tampines St 41
looking in while she did the honours. Or I could
simply do it at home. Which was what I decided
to do. And in style.

I wasn't planning to hide my bald head under
a hat or a wig every time someone came round
to visit. So I gathered my family members and
relatives around me for the occasion.

I felt it would be easier for them to accept my baldness if they saw me *getting* bald. Also, I didn't want my mum or my little nephew Reuben to have the shock of seeing me with hair one day and completely bald the next.

So during one of our Saturday evening get-togethers, after the dessert, we lined the floor with dog-eared, yellowed newspapers. My heart tumbled with a concoction of emotions as I sat on the white plastic kitchen stool Raja had set in the middle of the newspapers. I felt like a lamb led to the slaughter but I also felt an anointing of courage. It seemed so *final*! There was no turning back as Raja and Christina, my sister-in-law, took their positions and started work on my hair.

It was more difficult than we'd thought because I had fine hair but lots of it. Our tools were rather unprofessional. Disposable razors, a pair of fairly blunt stainless steel scissors (the kind we use for cutting paper) and Raja's little rusty scissors with grey plastic handles which he used for trim-ming his beard – our gift to him last Christmas.

They had to crop my curls as close as possible to the scalp before shaving them all off.

At first I sat upright, ready for whatever was to come. *Final or not – I'm ready for it*, I told myself. But as they continued I felt hair – my hair – fall onto my shoulders, arms, lap and onto the floor. I cringed and recoiled within and slouched even lower. My family must have sensed that for they immediately distracted me with pleasantries and kind jocularity. Just knowing that my family loved me and was supporting me gave me a big boost. I was drawn out of my misery and was even able to join in the fun for the rest of the ceremony.

When the job was done, I ran my fingers through my hair – I mean, over my head. It was a strange feeling because no hair slid through them. Just an uneven (thanks to my two amateur barbers!) prickly feeling. I looked at all the hair that had fallen onto the newspaper and held back tears. *I must be strong*, I told myself.

As I showered, I couldn't work up a rich lather as I used to. I really didn't need any shampoo at all. But it was easy to dry the scalp – and there were no irritating drips on the shoulders.

Then I braced myself and looked boldly in the mirror. My heart sank – I looked awful. I tried on the wig but ripped it off immediately because it simply wasn't me – even though we had gone looking for one that's supposed to look as close to my hairstyle as possible. I ran a comb over my head – I'm not sure for what reason, probably out of habit – and the painful reality sank in deeper.

Then Raja came upstairs to see how I was doing. I'm glad he did because I needed a shoulder to cry on. I cried softly in his arms. "You look fine," he said. I took courage in that. He even suggested shaving his head to keep me company. Naturally I protested – I mean, what would his company say with a fashion statement like that? I can just imagine him chairing meetings, and meeting clients without a strand of hair on his head. What a spectacle that will be!

When I came downstairs to meet the clan again, I felt rather self-conscious. Tiny trepidations about being bald haunted me but my family soon chased these shadows away, telling me how beautiful I looked after my pate had been washed and shined.

Hours after shaving my hair, we went to church for morning service. With the fuss it took to make my new look right, we arrived late. That was a mistake because it meant walking in to church when everyone else had been seated.

So there I was, walking self-consciously down the aisle, hand in hand with Raja, like a nervous bride. To my relief, we navigated to our usual seat without drawing too much attention. However, during the service, I had to consciously remember not to take off my hat when it felt hot or when my scalp got itchy.

I looked around and smiled at whoever met my eyes. Some gave an uncomfortable look and turned away not knowing how to respond. Good old Ivan did a double take and gave me a big smile. After the service, friends rallied round and said they liked the new look. For those who didn't quite know what to say, I'd say, "My hair was falling so I decided to shave it off…"

Meeting people for the first time that Sunday morning was not as frightful as I had thought.

So you can see why I wasn't ready for this priceless encounter in the afternoon when I rode in the car with four-year-old Eunice and her Mummy.

Eunice (who never ever speaks to me) asked:
"Mummy, why is Auntie Grace wearing a hat?"

Seeing Mummy in a fix, probably not wanting to
tell a fib, yet not knowing what to say, I quickly
replied: "I've got a hat on because it's hot." That
information must not have helped curious Eunice
much because when we were riding home at
10 pm that night, she asked: "Mummy, it's night
now so why is Auntie Grace still wearing a hat?"

This cookie is too smart for me, I thought, *I'd
better come clean*. So I said: "I've got no hair
that's why I'm wearing a hat." Immediately she
bolted straight up on her mother's lap, looked me
in the eye and said: "I want to see your head!"

*Give me a break, Eunice, I've only had this look
for a couple of hours and I'm still getting used
to it...*

Since Eunice's little lesson, I quickly learned that
how I dealt with my baldness determines other's
responses. So to put people at ease, I'd make
reference to my baldness nonchalantly, joke about
it, show them what was under the hat.

For the first couple of days, my head felt unusually
light. The nakedness made me feel vulnerable.

I had to remember not to reach for the hairbrush after my shower. I also had to remember to put on a hat when I was leaving the apartment. Early one morning while it was still dark, I dashed down the stairs of my apartment. As the chilly air caressed my head, I suddenly realised I'd forgotten to wear a hat! Thankfully, no one saw me.

Except for cold bareness I felt on my head, it was unexpectedly comfortable being bald. I soon got used to it and took to my new 'hairdo' like a fish to water.

We deal with our fears by taking control. By being mentally prepared. Share your fears with others. Remember, people love you for who you are, not for what you have (or do not have) on your head. Self-pity is not for the likes of us. Instead, we celebrate all things – including the 'light-headedness'– for a season. ✂

13 Oct 1998

Hi Mummy,
How's you doing? So you have started to wear your wig around, have you? Well, at least you don't have to worry about bad hair days. And besides many people want to shave their heads bald but don't have the guts. They would think you are very cool. Plus when it grows back it's gonna be even better. You know, maybe you should start listening to rock music so that you can have a compete image – funky hair & music.

Luff ya, Bessie

---

13 Oct 1998

Dear Friends,
As promised, my hair's beginning to fall. I love autumn BUT not when it's my hair that's falling! It's quite frightening actually...

Now what do I do when I'm hot and sweaty and I need to scratch my head while the wig is on? These are practical questions and I'll let you know how I do it discreetly after I've donned the wig for a couple of weeks.

Shall have to shave this weekend – I'll bring the family so that they are involved in the process. But I'll have to warn my hairdresser in case she goes into a state of shock (you know, rapid pulse, sweating, pallor, etc).

At least one person thinks I'm cool. Bessie emailed from Jakarta to tell me so (see email message above).

So it's not gonna be so bad after all. Not when I've so much support from everyone! I've got my wig (sometime between the liver scan and the bone scan appointments) because cancer or not, I'm going places.

Thank you for your prayers and continue to pray for me because the battle has only just begun. I leave you with these words of assurance from Isaiah 40:30,31
"Even youths grow tired and weary, and young men stumble and fall; but those who hope in the Lord shall renew their strength. They will soar on wings like eagles; They will run and not grow weary.
They will walk and not faint."

Take care and keep in touch!
Grace

Bald Encounters

Life goes on even when you have no hair on your head. So I was soon meeting people at the usual shops, market and restaurants. What's really funny was how people took to my new look.

One night I craved for a cup of hot chrysanthemum tea. So we drove over to the nearest *kopitiam**. As I tried to give my order in Penang Hokkien, the old man making the drinks kept making fun of my order and feigning that he couldn't understand what I'd wanted. I repeated my order in Hokkien and English.

Reluctantly, he pulled up a cup with chrysanthemum powder and as he was pouring hot water into it, he asked me rather abruptly: "What! You Chinese or *ang moh***?" I felt provoked and was

---

* *Kopitiam* is a transliteration of the Hokkien word for coffeeshop.
** *Ang moh* is literally "red hair" in Hokkien, a term used to refer to a Caucasian.

about to respond when I put my hand to my head and realised that I had a hat on. It wasn't the accent after all, it was the hat.

I like it when people are comfortable with the fact that I have cancer, like our friendly taxi drivers in Singapore. I'd flagged a cab and told the driver I wanted to go to Borders. Peering at me through the rear mirror, he said, "You look like tourist." *Oh no, it's my hat again,* I thought. "No, I'm not a tourist. I'm wearing a hat because all my hair has dropped. I'm on cancer treatment."

"Don't mind, ah, how much you pay for your chemo, ah?" he asked briskly. After I told him the fees I paid, he said, "I hope you don't mind I tell you this. My friend's mother, ah, she got cancer but she died, you know. Little while after they tell her she got cancer, she die already…"

So much for positive thinking.

The Pasta Fresca Da Salvatore at the East Coast is one of our favourite eateries. I felt I had to let Alias, the assistant manager, know about my condition, and especially about my baldness, in case my hat fell off in the restaurant one of these days.

He came by when we asked for
more chili, and asked us if the
Arrabiata wasn't hot enough. I grabbed the
opportunity and said nonchalantly, "I'm on
chemotherapy and my tastebuds are blunted, so I
need food to be very strong and *pedas**." And
quickly added that my hair has fallen that's why
I'm wearing a hat. Anyone else would have
thought this a weird conversation but good old
Alias took the cue and we moved on to a very
technical discussion about Medisave.

Our friends provided constant encouragement
during my hairless days. Karen sent an email to
say that God loves me so much He knows the
number of hairs on my head. And there's the joke
about how God made beautiful heads – the rest
He covered with hair.

At home we had fun too. I was the butt of the
family's *botak*** jokes but never in an unkind
way. Raja and Bessie would sometimes give my
prickly head a loving rub or plant a kiss on it
when I'm feeling down.

A few months after I shaved my head, we were to
take a flight to visit Bessie in Jakarta. This would
be my first flight since my diagnosis and I was a

---

*   *Pedas* is Malay for spicy.
** *Botak* is Malay for bald head.

bit apprehensive about wearing a hat on board. What if the stewardess were to announce: "During takeoff and landing, please fasten your seatbelts, keep your seats upright and take off your hats..." Then I thought, *That'd be fun and I'd have a field day... I wonder if the other passengers and crew are able to handle my botak head?*

Anyway, the night before we travelled, I asked Raja if I should don the wig (which I'd never used before) instead of the hat. "CERTAINLY NOT!" he said, "I might get a shock!"

So you see, I had fun with my bald pate. Still, I can't deny the trauma of losing all my hair. Many people can handle anything but this. It is the reality that keeps reminding you of the cancer. So you learn to deal with it.

The first step is acceptance, I tell myself. *Accept the fact that you are bald.* I use my baldness as a reminder that I am doing something about the cancer. As I undergo chemotherapy the drugs will destroy the cancer cells. Unfortunately, the drugs also cause the hair to fall out. So my lack of hair is evidence that I am fighting the good fight.

Then I learn to live with it. There are many aids to help a person cope with being bald. Hats, caps,

wigs, scarves, bandanas – I had fun
with these and took the opportunity
to make a fashion statement.

I wasn't merely going to make the
best of a bad situation, I wanted
to enjoy it as well.

Hi Doc, It's Me Again

Finding the 'right' oncologist is important. You have to place your life in his hands. It must be someone you trust. He is the supporter, your cheerleader. The conscience that keeps you honest. He lifts your spirits when you are down. But he talks to you about your condition with no holds barred.

It was a given who my oncologist was going to be. Six months earlier, I'd profiled him for a regional health magazine. Upon discovering the lump in my breast, I emailed him from Jakarta. I was not even sure if he was going to respond to the email – after all we had only been in touch for the interview.

My oncologist surprised us when he did more than just respond – he called me in Jakarta and asked me to go straight to his clinic as soon as I landed in Singapore that evening. He would wait for me.

We were impressed because he needn't have gone out of his way to assist us. We felt cared for. In the tumble of emotions, we needed the sane voice of authority to steady our nerves and help us think. My oncologist provided that anchor.

I knew a lot *about* my oncologist from the interview he gave me, but I didn't know him well until he became my physician. The frequent trips to his office during my chemo treatment gave Raja and I a chance to know him better as a person. We soon became friends.

Although he said we could call him, we seldom used that privilege unless it was an emergency. So email was our regular channel of communication. He could read the messages and reply them at leisure.

Email messages began to fly back and forth soon after my first cycle of chemo...

---

5 Oct 1998

Hi,

I hope that things haven't been too bad since we last met. Be prepared for Week 2 when the hair falls. Despite all that I say, it will come as a bit of a shock. The other thing to look out for is fever. Call me if you have any temperature above 38 degrees Centigrade. OK, back to seeing patients. Keep well and God bless.

Wow! my oncologist sent me an email. I was
thrilled! He actually cared enough to write me.

And so I took the liberty to write him about
things pertaining to cancer and its treatment.
I figured that if he didn't want to read those he
could trash them. I believe he replied *every* email
I sent him.

When I started becoming a hypochondriac and
began to experience every possible symptom –
*I think I've got urine infection; I feel lousy physi-
cally, nauseous, bloated. I feel pregnant* – he sent
me this:

Cheer up! There's nothing wrong with you and
you're going to beat the damn cancer.

I guess I needed that to put me in perspective and
get me out of my moping spirit.

My chemo required three doses every 21-day
cycle. So for three consecutive days every 21
days, I'd have to go for injections. The problem
was my veins were fragile. We tried using the
branula hoping to keep it there for all three days,
but we always had to change that on the third
day because the veins would go into spasms and
the drugs could not be administered.

Moreover, only my right hand could be used – my left hand had its lymph nodes removed so we couldn't do any procedure there as there was no protection from infection. It was torturous having to be pricked over and over again for blood tests and injections, and that only on my right arm.

The good doc then suggested that I "do what VIP's do – insert a portacath", that is have a tube inserted directly to the heart through which drugs can be administered. "Sure," I said, and proceeded to see my surgeon about it. I thought it would be a simple procedure that would be done under local anaesthesia (LA).

When my surgeon said that I had to do it under general anaesthesia (GA), I freaked out. After agonising over it, I decided go into confession with my oncologist.

---

11 Oct 1998

Hi Doc,

I've got a confession to make. When I saw the surgeon, he told me that the port has to be inserted under GA. I'm really afraid to go through GA again and will only do so if it is necessary to save my life.

Here's why I dread GA:

Fear 1: I hate to come out of GA feeling the hard airway in my throat.

Fear 2: I hate to come out of GA feeling the pain of the wound.

Fear 3: I hate the sick feeling that follows GA, and the very, very sore throat.

Fear 4: What if I DON'T come out of GA — then I won't be able to say goodbye to my family and friends?

Fear 5: What if they give me insufficient GA so that I appear to be asleep but I know what's going on around me and feel the pain?

AAAhhhhhhhhhhhhh! No GA p-l-e-a-s-e!!!

I went though the motion of signing the pre-op papers and making the appointment. But deep down inside I was beginning to feel like a sick person for the first time. The fears are so real, I have nightmares about them. So I've decided I don't want to be a VIP and have a port because I don't want GA.

I'm working on my right hand to make it strong and the veins prominent. I have started using Raja's exercise grip. I can barely move it 1 cm but by the time I'm through, my right hand will be stronger than Rambo's and no one's going to insult my veins any more.

So can we postpone putting in the port until it becomes crucial? I want to have a go with what veins I've got first.

I hope you will support me as we work through this veins dilemma together.

Your poor patient

Here's the reply:

---

12 Oct 1998

Dear Rambo
I hear you loud and clear. If you really don't want the port, then we shall make do with your Rambo-like veins. Call me.

How's that for a funny doctor? Incidentally, my right hand did not quite match Rambo's, but I did manage to stave off the portacath, and complete the eight cycles of chemo using the veins on my right hand.

I believe my oncologist's humour, accessibility, and warmth made a lot of difference to my treatment and recovery. His outgoing personality brought cheer to an otherwise morbid situation. We had our serious discussions about treatment options and the like, but we also had great fun discussing things other than cancer. His openness meant that I could ask him anything, and that gave me peace of mind.

I would not have hesitated to change doctors if I had not been comfortable with or confident of my oncologist whom I see as the head of the medical team. I have no doubts concerning his knowledge or expertise. As visiting consultant to a restructured hospital, he meets with the oncology team once a week to discuss cases and keep abreast of cancer research and treatment.

Often, it's a matter of chemistry whether you get on with your doctor or not. I'm glad that we did with mine. The diagnosis of cancer was difficult enough to handle; we didn't need problems getting along with the person who was going to manage it.

While a good doctor-patient relationship is important, you also need to read up on the disease and learn as much as possible about it. Be interested in the treatment, be inquisitive. Communicate. Take responsibility for your treatment. You don't have to agree with everything the doctor says.

Oncologists cost a lot. If you can, go for the best. We've heard horror stories of tumours that were allowed to grow because surgery had to be delayed due to lack of facility. The person progressed from Stage I of the disease to Stage II in a matter of weeks while waiting for the scheduled surgery. We've heard of uncaring doctors who do more harm by their words than the cancer does.

However, oncologists are human too. With the steep rise in cancer patients in Singapore, oncologists here can become overworked and may sometimes be testy. Dealing with death takes its toll. We have to live with some failings. But if possible, find someone who has time for you, who treats you as a person, not just as a patient with a dreaded disease.

I was lucky.

I still see my oncologist once every two months. He hasn't lost his humour yet.

Thanks, doc, for everything.

Instant Celebrity

One day I woke up with an excruciating, gritty pain in my left eye. It was swollen and so photophobic I couldn't open it at all. It was Sunday and no ophthalmologist was available. So we went to the neighbourhood GP who treated me for conjunctivitis and gave me antibiotic eye drops.

When it didn't get better the next day, I went to see an ophthalmologist. He examined the inside of the eye and immediately ordered me to visit a doctor at the restructured hospital who specialised in cornea and infective eye diseases.

Something was seriously wrong.

The eye specialist at the restructured hospital looked into the eye and said that there was a white immunity ring and ulceration. All of a sudden, I became an instant celebrity.

One ophthalmologist after another came by to look at the white immunity ring.

"OK, just relax. Don't close your eye," they'd say. "The light's too bright is it? OK, I'll use the lower light."

In order to cooperate with the doctors, I'd pry the left eye open with my hands but it would lacrimate so much I gave up. The eye was so sensitive to light, it wouldn't stay open.

"OK, let me put some drops into the eye to dilate it," the doctor said, breathing onto my face, and then continued peering into the eye while I struggled to keep it open in the bright light.

After the entire eye department had "oohed" and "ahhed" over the immunity ring, the ophthalmologist gave me the bottom line – they didn't know what caused it. They suspected virus, parasite or fungus which had become active due to my low immunity. To confirm this, the doctor took scrapes from the cornea to culture the microorganism. It would take 48 hours or more for the results to be available.

While the celebrity status was rather enjoyable, with all the 'big guns' of the ophthalmology department fussing over my cornea, it was also frightening. If they didn't know what it was, then they wouldn't know how to treat it.

My heart sank.

After putting their heads together again, they finally decided to take a chance and treat it as a viral infection. But before they would let me off, I had to go for a photo session. They needed to take slides of the white immunity ring "so that medical students can benefit from looking at it." I struggled to pry my eye open in the bright light as the technician took a couple of shots.

As I was leaving, she bent over and whispered in my ear, "I won't charge you for taking the pictures." I whispered back, "OK. Thanks." She must be crazy if she'd expected me to pay for the slides that "medical students were going to benefit from." I didn't request for them in the first place. In fact I thought the hospital should pay me for donating pictures of the immunity ring in my eye.

The bill, excluding the slides which were other-wise chargeable if not for the kindness of the technician, came to a hefty four hundred bucks. "The cultures are expensive," the cashier apologetically said, even without my asking. The irony of it was that after paying so much for an afternoon's consultation, the doctors – senior consultants all – still didn't know what I was suffering from for certain.

So with an eye pad ($5!) strapped to my left eye after it had been dressed and antibiotic cream (another $5!) applied to prevent the scraped area from getting septic, I went home. I had come with two eyes and left with only one. Plus a big dent in the pocket.

The culture for parasites came back negative. The culture for virus came back unclear. So they took blood for further viral tests and another scrape from the cornea for fungus.

As it turned out, they had taken the right decision to treat the infection as viral, though there were no clear signs and symptoms. My eye eventually cleared up with the medication.

Unfortunately the virus lies dormant and springs to life from time to time when my immunity is low. Which is quite often.

2 Feb 1999

Dear friends,
Thanks for your prayers. It is comforting to know that
you are praying for me. My prayer now is that it will
not spread to the other eye. Right now I'm One-Eyed
Jack; I'd hate to be No-Eyed Jack.

We are so weary. It's just been one infection after
another. Please pray that God will break this pattern
of infections which are but distractions – so that we
can concentrate on treating the cancer. That God will
give us strength and hope and like Job we will come
out unscathed and triumphant eventually. That these
trials will become testimonies for Him.

Keep in touch and God bless
Grace

3 Feb 1999

Dear friends,
Just came back from the hospital. The ophthalmologist says that the cornea is getting better – less
swelling. He was excited that I could read some of
the huge numbers on the eye chart. So am I! The
largest number 5 is still blur but it is more visible

than during the previous visit. The doctor still doesn't know what is causing the problem — there was no viral growth on the culture (yet). Took some blood for further viral tests.

The healing has begun and we are praying that God will bring it to completion. So too for the breast cellulitis which has not completely subsided yet. Please continue to pray for the primary concern (which is the cancer) — that God will grant the oncologist wisdom as to when to proceed with the chemo in the midst of these infections. And that the delay in administering it will not make any difference to the effectiveness of the treatment.

Shalom
Grace

One Step Forward, Two Steps Back

When I was undergoing chemo, I had my fair share of infections. Timing is everything when it comes to susceptibility to infection. There is a period in the chemo cycle when the white blood cells would plunge. The medical term for this is 'neutropenia'. For Taxol – the chemotherapy I was prescribed – neutropenia falls between Day 5 and Day 10. I was especially conscious of this period of the cycle.

You hope you don't catch a bug around the time chemo is to be administered. Because that would mean the infection could escalate during neutropenia, just when you need white blood cells most to fight the infection.

And because your resistance is lowered during neutropenia, you don't want to travel or be in crowds where you might catch a bug. So you confine yourself to the safety of the home and do homey things like reading and sewing. And you don't want to cut yourself either. This is because your platelets are low and you tend to bleed more during this period. Moreover, open wounds might allow germs to enter the body and cause infection.

As Day 10 passes, you relax a little, and can't wait to go out again. But you also worry that you may have caught something during neutropenia, and you begin looking for symptoms. You wait a couple of days and when there are no signs you breathe easier. Then you've got a week to live normally before the cycle starts all over again. It's like tightrope walking.

I took all the precautions and still managed to develop an abscess in the armpit, left breast cellulitis, folliculitis and yeast infection on the scalp and a chest infection. I was told the first two were probably due to bacteria which were already in the blood and were therefore not 'caught' from someone else. The folliculitis could have been due to the steroids given as premedication for the chemo, which suppresses immunity. The yeast is resident on everyone's body but multiplies when the body's resistance drops. The chest infection was the only infection I could have caught from someone.

It was bad enough with the physical side effects of chemo. But further battering from infection made life unbearable. The high fever, the throbbing pain, the bag of pus in the axilla (where my lymph nodes had been removed); the fear of going under general anaesthesia to clear up the infection; the daily torturous dressings that required flushing out and plugging with a whole roll of ribbon gauze, and messy leaking lymphatic fluids; the hard tensed pain of cellulitis of the breast and more. All of these made me lapse, in weaker moments, into self-pity.

As though to add insult to injury, the infections and operations caused the chemo treatment to be delayed. Hence the entire course of eight cycles took much longer than expected. As with any cancer patient, I had a burning desire to get chemo done and over with. But with the frequent bouts of infection, I often felt like I was taking one step forward, two steps back. I did not seem to be making any progress.

The withdrawal of high dosages of steroid, given as premedication every cycle, caused eczema to blaze in with a vengeance.

I felt like Job with the dreadful sores, wondering when the suffering was ever going to end.

"How long more, O Lord," I'd cry. "I don't think I can take this much longer." But I always did. I assure you the strength did not come from me; it came from God.

The infections forced me to be laid up at home, too exhausted to even do simple tasks. A very frustrating thing for me especially when I yearned to go for my morning walks, or to just sit by the seaside, or potter around the bookstore, or write. I dreaded the four walls; the coldness of the empty apartment with our stuff put away in boxes for the move to Jakarta which never materialised.

I was even too ill to read, so I did the only thing I could do – listen to music and devotional narrations while lying in bed. The music soothed and the devotions lifted my sagging spirit.

I learnt during these periods of rest that it was alright to be doing nothing. It was a very difficult lesson to learn since I am a person who must constantly be doing something or other.

Since I have gotten well, I have removed those CD's and cassettes from my collection. Listening to them brings back too many memories of the illness. I never want to play them again because they remind me so much of the pain I went through.

Doing a Dolly Parton Again

S
o there I was, a regular hospital bird, being admitted to hospital every couple of weeks because of infection.

Unlike Raja, I did not find the hospital repulsive; it did not reek of death to me. I suppose I feel at home in hospitals because I had spent so much time walking its floors as a staff nurse.

Whenever I was admitted, I'd ask Raja to tell our friends I didn't want visitors. I really wasn't up to it. The body was exhausted and battered, the mind dulled by the physical pain, and my spirits low. But inevitably with every admission, friends would come to see me. At the end of their visit, I was always glad they came because they brought me cheer and prayed with me.

During one of my hospitalisations for cellulitis of the breast, I was admitted for at least a week.

The fever refused to subside and my left breast refused to return to its normal size.

The oncologist and the surgeon could not figure out the problem. They had never quite seen the likes of this before – it didn't get better with the antibiotics but it didn't get worse either. A 'normal' cellulitis would have cleared after a week of strong antibiotics.

Everyday the surgeon would examine the breast to see if it was fluctuant. If it was, then he could operate and drain the pus. But the breast remained hard and swollen. There was nothing to drain, so an operation was not necessary.

After observing the infection for a couple of days, the surgeon said: "Let's try magnesium sulphate dressing."

"That's ancient," I protested. I had used that for my patients aeons ago when practising nursing. "We have to use every weapon in the armamentarium," he told me. So we marched boldly into battle with new ammunition.

Frustrated at the non-progress, the oncologist joked: "We should have lopped off the breast in the first place, then we wouldn't have this problem…" We all had a much-needed laugh over that.

Finally, the temperature unexpectedly returned to normal and the swelling subsided somewhat. Everyone heaved a sigh of relief. We attributed that to the grace of God. The doctors were more than pleased to send me packing home once the temperature remained normal for 48 hours.

In the meantime, however, my friends were having fun at my expense.

Jennifer, when she came to visit, nonchalantly asked: "Grace… did you pray for big breasts?" She kept such a straight face that I burst out laughing. "No Jennifer, I didn't. And if I did, I would have asked for two!" I retorted.

I called Karen to tell her that I had been admitted for another breast infection. After describing the anatomical presentation, she asked laughingly: "Oh no, are you doing a Dolly Parton again?"

Subsequently that phrase stuck. So whenever there was a breast infection, I'd call up friends and say: "Hi guys, I'm doing a Dolly Parton again." And they'd all know exactly what I meant.

Eternity in a Prom Dress

Bessie was back home from Jakarta during Christmas break. She had a mission to accomplish on this trip back to Singapore. To buy a prom dress.

You must understand something about Bessie and prom dresses. Or any dress for that matter. It has to be perfect. The colour, the length, the cutting and the fabric have to be just right. This made the search for *the* prom dress tantamount to the quest for the Holy Grail.

Bessie was studying at the British International School (BIS) of Jakarta then and being in Year 11, she was to go to the prom in February. It had been about two and half months since I started chemo. I was recovering from an operation to drain and clean up an abscess which had formed in the axilla where the lymph nodes had been removed. My white blood counts were so low

I had to have injections to prop them up. I also had to defer my next round of chemo because of this. As you can imagine, I was tired, listless, easily upset. Certainly not the best companion for such an adventure.

But nothing was going to stop me from helping my 15 year-old choose her first prom dress. I had strong reasons for it.

Early one morning we set off down Orchard Road going from store to store, shop to shop, from one end of the road to the other.

Christmas was in the air. The bright red and green decorations brought cheer, but the crowds didn't. Orchard Road was swarming with people. Jostling our way through sweaty crowds, we became increasingly stressed as we sifted through hundreds of pretty possibilities, but none that matched Bessie's idea of *the* prom dress. There were plenty of flimsy black numbers with spaghetti straps but they were not appropriate for her "because they are too common, too revealing and lacked character."

By mid afternoon, we were exhausted and very edgy. All the food outlets were full to overflowing, we could hardly find a spot to rest our throbbing feet.

We came home that day empty-handed. Depressed, Bessie stayed in bed the rest of the day. When I checked in on her that night, she was angry with the whole world. Everything was going wrong: Why did she have to be alone in Jakarta? Why did mummy have to have cancer? Why couldn't she find a decent prom dress? What if she couldn't find a decent prom dress before the prom?

I promised her that everything would be alright and that we'd go shopping tomorrow. "I'll go alone," she said. She was adamant about not letting me go with her because she assumed that my frayed nerves were due to my reluctance to go shopping. I felt she was punishing me because I used to hate going shopping with her.

Her reaction made me wonder. Was this only about a dress? Or was it subconscious rebellion? Hidden anger. The unfairness of it all – the intolerable burden on tender teenage shoulders.

It's true I disliked shopping. I found it terribly tiring going from shop to shop, aimlessly almost. But that was before I had cancer. Now my days are numbered. And this noble quest for a prom dress was something I wanted very much to do, however tiring it was, however long it would take. It meant a lot for me to be involved in this major event.

I broke down and wept, and told her: "I want to come with you to buy your dress because I may not be here next year to help you choose the dress for your next prom."

There was a pregnant silence before she broke down and wept inconsolably. She hugged me and said "Mummy I don't want you to die." It was the first time she's ever spoken about my dying. She had been the strong one when I was diagnosed. She remained positive and was a tower of strength for us when Raja and I were devastated.

And now for the first time, the fragile façade was broken and we were able to talk about her fears and her pain. With six lymph nodes affected, the odds of a recurrence were pretty high. There was no guarantee, and I did not give her any. Except to say that God is control and that we shall leave it in His hands.

Finally honesty shone through. We were able to talk, with no holds barred, about life, about death, about eternity. About the things in life that really mattered.

When crisis, such as cancer strikes, everyone puts on a façade and wears masks. Both the victim and the family members. We take on new roles.

We repress our anger – mostly for the sake of others. We put on a brave front when there's really a need for grieving and coming to terms with the situation. We need to release our fears, to be open and transparent. It is in sharing that we can come to terms with the pain and the burden.

The next day we continued our search for Bessie's dream dress. To her delight, she found it at Robinson's. It was perfect. A charming blue crepe dress – her favourite colour – long and elegant in a bias cut. The delicate silver threads glistened when light fell on them. She looked gorgeous in it. There was a lump in my throat and I held back tears as I watched her turn this way and that in front of the full length mirror in the store. Then she looked at me, her face beaming and said, "Mummy, I like this dress. It's lovely." And indeed it was.

Of course, then we had to look for shoes... not just any shoes, but *matching* shoes. So we soldiered on...

When Raja came back in the evening, the living room was converted into a catwalk. Bessie descended slowly from the stairs all dressed up. I could see the pride in Papa's eyes as he beamed at his little girl, now transformed into a young lady. Perhaps it's time to buy a double-barrel shotgun in case the boys started swarming the place…

* * *

Even as I write this a year has slipped by and we've just bought another dress for this year's prom. This one's a two-piece maroon organza. We did the honours when we came back for my oncologist's visit. I was glad to have been involved again this year. Living in hope and trust, I look forward to next year's ball… and the ones after that.

Thanks Mum!

Depression

The dark brooding mood comes insidiously. I usually realise that something is wrong after there's been a blow-up or two. For days I'd be hovering around the edge of the 'dark pit', as I call the depression. All it takes to topple me into it is a feather.

Once in it, it's almost impossible to come out. I think the cruelest thing for a person to say to one who is in depression is "Snap out of it." If she could, she would. "Cheer up" is not very helpful either. Picture someone standing on solid ground, arms akimbo, saying to a person sinking in mire, "Hey you, get out of there!" That's just what it's like.

What causes the depression? I don't really know. Some say it's due to the chemical imbalance caused by chemo. Others blame it on the hormones.

While others say it's everything put together –
the trauma of the diagnosis, the treatment,
the hormones.

Whatever the cause, the person in depression
needs a lot of support. In my case, I needed plenty
of hugs and assurance. When the family took my
angry words personally and reacted to them
(which, by the way, is a most natural thing to do),
I felt rejected and sank deeper into the dark pit.
I wanted them to help me and tell me it's alright
and that they love me though I was behaving so
repugnantly. I longed to make them understand
that I wanted to help myself but couldn't, that I
hated being depressed as much as they did.

But, I found admitting my need terribly humiliat-
ing. It was difficult asking for a hug, or telling
them I'm falling into the pit, that I needed conces-
sions for the next couple of days until I 'snap out
of it'. So I would put off telling them anything at
all. I wanted them to recognise the signs and give
me the help I needed without my asking for it.
But they usually didn't and the situation inevitably got worse.

It must have been very trying for the family to
help me when I was depressed. I often grieve for
time wasted when I was in the pit. I have learnt

that I should recognise depression as early as possible and to tell the family what's happening before any damage is done.

On top of depression, I felt anger. Anger that was so tangible I could touch it. I'd never known such anger in my life before. I had no control over the anger; I thought I was going mad. Like a person possessed, I would scream until my lungs hurt. Then I'd be filled with remorse and guilt at having hurt the person I had directed my anger at.

Sometimes I would become violent. I'd grab whatever was within reach and smash it against the wall. Violent scenes, over which I had no control, would play in my mind. One night, when that happened, I got up, went downstairs and took the chopper from the kitchen drawer. I wrapped it in newspaper, went outside and threw it in the rubbish dump. I was afraid of what I might do to hurt myself or my family when I became angry.

I emailed my doctor when I was going through all of this. Told him I needed help. See a psychiatrist, perhaps. He scheduled an appointment after office hours for us to see him two days later.

The next day, the moods and depression had disappeared. I was whole again and indefatigable. Ready for whatever life chose to throw at me.

I cancelled the appointment and braced myself for the next round of depression. I was determined, however, to live life to the max until depression visited me again.

When I saw my doctor a week later for my chemo, he said, "Been grumpy lately, eh?"

That, I thought, was the understatement of the century.

* * *

It's been a year since I completed chemo and radiation. God isn't finished with me yet. I'm still under construction. While I still have bouts of moods and depression, they are, fortunately, not as frequent nor as intense as they were during chemo. The family is working on it. So am I.

Menopause

"Mummy, the doctor says no more periods – does that mean no more premenstrual syndrome?" asked Bessie as soon as we stepped out of the oncologist's office. I thought I saw a flicker of hope in her eyes. Premenstrual syndrome (PMS), you see, is life threatening at our home.

One of the things chemotherapy does to the female body is to bring on the onset of menopause. Initially, the diagnosis and the immediate commencement of chemo treatment preoccupied me so much I didn't have time to ponder the implications of menopause. As I settled into the routine of treatment, the signs and symptoms of menopause crept up on me.

The loss of oestrogen caused many parts of the body to shrivel and dry up. That was exactly how I felt: old, shrivelled and dried up. Like a preserved prune.

I had always hoped to grow old gracefully. No hang ups about the *rite de passage* and growing old. But then I was banking on that happening at 50. So when menopause rushed in at 41, I grieved the loss of my youth (or rather, middle age), and what could have been another nine years or so of bleeding associated with fertility and womanhood.

For someone whose period was never much of an inconvenience and who celebrated her woman-hood every month, menopause was a bitter pill. This was the fifth blow since I found the lump. First the diagnosis, then six positive lymph nodes, third the separation from my daughter who had to go to Jakarta alone to continue her schooling while Raja and I remained in Singapore to commence treatment, fourth the chemotherapy and loss of hair, and now, menopause.

But I soon realised that menopause was not an issue at all. The choice was between menopause and life, and periods and an early death. Not much of a choice, really.

As things fell into perspective, I accepted my lot of an early menopause. I was determined to live with the inconvenient symptoms and overcome the emotional hang-ups that surround menopause.

But it was not easy.

"Raja, do you feel hot?" I kept hearing myself ask over and again soon after I'd started chemo. He was the perfect thermostat because he was not affected by hormonal changes. If he says it's hot, then it's the environment that's hot and humid, and we'd turn the airconditioning down. If he said no then I knew it was the hot flushes; we'd turn down the airconditioning anyway. It's amazing how Raja didn't freeze to death.

After a while I learned to recognise the hot flushes and stopped asking him about the weather. The hot flushes and sweating created havoc with my eczema.

The damp caused by sweat made my skin itch badly. Weals appeared all over especially in the places with crevices such as the back of the elbows and knees. To make it more bearable, I wore old thin baggy cotton T-shirts and cotton shorts. I'd sit in front of a fan or in an airconditioned room for

most part of the day. To cool off, I'd step under
a cold shower many times a day.

I stopped cooking because the heat from the stove
made the skin worse, especially my face which gets
most of the heat. I stopped vigorous exercises in
the gym because my face and the body would heat
up. The itch would get so bad I'd scratch till the
flesh became raw. In the place of workouts at the
gym I took long walks at dawn and night time.

Menopause also caused insomnia. Life became
one long cycle of wakefulness, and that added
stress to my life.

I'd lie in bed tossing and turning, afraid that I
might wake Raja. I would eventually fall asleep
towards dawn – when it was time to get up.
I made it a point to get up no matter how tired
I was because I wanted to see Raja before he left
for work as I wouldn't see him again till evening.

I'd then try to keep awake all day so that I could
sleep at night. But when night came, my body
would be exhausted but I still couldn't sleep as
my mind, albeit hazy, would be working over-
time. Needless to say, I was grouchy and grumpy
most of the time.

The stress caused by insomnia made the eczema flare up. Doctors tried to give me tranquillisers and sleeping pills but they didn't work too well on me – they made me fall into a spell of fitful sleep which would last only about an hour. My semi-conscious mind would be troubled with horrible dreams. I couldn't recall the last time I had a good night's rest. How I longed for a good night's rest, for *just one night*.

The most difficult thing about menopause were the volatile moods and depression. It was worse than PMS which had been a serious problem at home. At its worst, my husband threatened to divorce me each time it flared, and my daughter threatened to check me into a hotel room until I came out of it. I often wished I could crawl under a little carton box and remain there until the depression passed.

I soon found that there was a pattern to my moods, even in menopause. I was edgy, fragile and given to tears, and prone to depression every three or four weeks. It was as though there was still a hormonal cycle although there was no period to show for it. I learned to enjoy and maximise the good days. The bad days, however, were hell – for me and especially for the family.

Dr Mariam Stoppard in her book 'Menopause' says "If you have suffered from PMS all your life, you are more likely to experience intensified symptoms as you become menopausal" – I guess I was the perfect candidate for that.

The symptoms of menopause not only affect women physically and emotionally but also intellectually. In my case, it was forgetfulness. I often forget what I was going to say, mid-sentence. My thought processes seem to get short-circuited all the time.

I forget where I put things. Often I tell myself I'd put something 'right here' so that I won't forget, but I'd forget where 'right here' was. I resorted to writing things on the white board at my desk or making an entry in my diary or notebook. Trouble was, I had so many diaries and note-books, I couldn't remember which one I'd written the information in.

It was frustrating to keep backtracking because I had forgotten to bring an address or the shopping list. I kept hearing myself say, "Must be getting old." It was painful when the fact sunk in.

Coping with the symptoms of menopause is bad enough. Slip cancer into the picture – its diagnosis and treatment – and living seems a herculean task. Menopause is one more facet of reality you have to come to terms with; its symptoms – some more daunting than others – one more thing to learn to live with.

You need to give yourself time to grieve the loss of womanhood. And to give yourself time to adjust to the changes in your life. With time and help from the family, you will learn to accept and learn to live with menopause.

Time is always a healer, and your family the best medicine, at this stage in your life.

Any More Sambal Petai, Nur?

The common belief goes that people lose weight when they're on chemotherapy. Sad accounts of vomiting, nausea, and loss of appetite associated with chemo treatment abound.

I'm almost ashamed to say that not only was I able to keep my food down, I ate so well I put on weight. A lot of it.

Every time I went to see my oncologist, he'd check my weight. And every time it would inevitably go up. I thought chemotherapy would help me get down to the weight I desired. Fat hope (pun not intended)!

After a couple of visits, I pre-empted the weight increase by saying, "Doc, I've put on weight again" even before I stepped on the weighing scale.

"Why are you so fat?" he cheekily asked as he stepped over from his desk to read the scales.

"I want to eat all the time and I haven't been exercising," I'd say.

"Why haven't you been exercising," he'd continue, trying to suppress a mischievous smile.

I ignored him. I've just had surgery to drain the huge abscess in the axilla and I'm still recovering, that's why. And he knew it but he pleaded ignorance by being silly. I guess he had a point to make too – chemo was no excuse for irresponsible eating and careless neglect of exercise.

In his saner moments during the consultation, he told me: "That's how we like our patients who are on chemo." What he meant, of course, was that it was better to be able to eat and stay nourished than not to be able to eat.

Chemo leaves a perpetual metallic taste on my tongue. I had a dire need to dull that awful taste so I continuously chewed on very strong, sharp-tasting snacks – extra salty *sng buay**, extra sour pickles, and my favourite, Marks and Spencers' Fizzy Lemon Fish.

---

* *Sng buay* is the Hokkien name for preserved prunes.

The economy was pretty slow at that time but you could say I single-handedly kept the snack industry buoyant. As you can see, the effort did not go fruitless; the economy has rebounded.

I always carried some pickles or sweets with me in my bag to help me tide over long periods of time on the road. Friends would bring all sorts of sour plums, sweets and the like, when they visited. And there was always a containerful in the oncologist's office.

The drugs also took away the ability to taste. Everything tasted flat. I needed more sugar, more salt, more tamarind. I'd yearn for sour Penang *laksa** or fish head curry, and I got my helper Nur to cook her spicy Indonesian *sambals***. The stronger the flavour the better, so we often had potent stuff like *sambal petai*. Made with *chili padi*. The Jallehs would invite us over for their renowned fiery 'devil curry' and *assam**** fish.

May Chee, whose brother-in-law had completed chemo treatment, felt she understood precisely what I was going through. Being a staff nurse, she admonished me for going out unnecessarily to buy food for fear of catching infection.

* *laksa* is rice noodle cooked in a spicy soup.
** *Sambal* is a special chili paste made with various spices.
***Assam is a spicy, sour-tasting dish usually made from chili paste and the rind of tamarind.

So she dropped by regularly with different types of breakfast after her marketing.

She would cull from our conversations what I craved for, and behold, the next morning that very food will be sitting on the table when I came down for breakfast. Like manna from heaven. Whatever else she brought, there was always soya bean milk and soya bean curd – "because you need the protein," she'd fondly say.

On strategic days of the chemo cycle when the blood counts were up and it was safe for me to go out, we'd go gallivanting around town. One day it would be for 'the longest buffet' in town, another day it'd be a simple *tosai** and sweet *teh tarik*** in Serangoon Road.

With the loss of taste, I'd feel like I had not eaten even though I'd just finished a full meal. Often I'd ask for something to eat 10 minutes after a meal. Although my stomach said "full" my brain said "empty" as I had not tasted anything and was therefore not satiated. It was awful being full to bursting and yet keeling over with hunger. The perpetual request for this or that food drove the helper crazy.

* *Tosai* is a savoury Indian pancake made from ground urad dhall.
** *Teh tarik* is tea with milk, concocted by pouring it from one cup into another, till a frothy foam forms on the top.

It didn't help that chemotherapy slows down metabolic rate. Here I was stuffing myself and my body couldn't burn it off fast enough. So whenever I felt well enough, I would walk 6 to 11 km a day to burn off the calories. But my expenditure could never keep up with my intake. Hence the kilograms piled on.

Sometimes I'd look at myself in the mirror and exclaim to Raja, "Bad enough that I am bald, why do I also have to be so fat!" He'd give me a hug and say: "I like you fat; there's more of you to hug!"

Looking back, I think, as a rule, you should eat well when you are able to because there will be times when you can't. During chemo, there were times when I couldn't eat at all such as when I was very ill with an infection or when I was in pain when the axilla filled up with lymphatic fluid.

There's of course always the danger of getting carried away with undisciplined eating. However, being on chemo doesn't give one the license to eat *ad lib*. While it is not the time to take on other problems like obesity or cholesterol, you also don't want to eat as though your whole life depended on it and burden yourself with other health problems.

Moderation, I think, is the goal. Although only those who've been through chemo would know how difficult that is when your tastebuds just would not behave themselves. The spirit is often willing, the flesh sadly weak.

I put on an extra 5 kg when I was on chemo. A year after chemo was completed, I lost 9 kg. That was the lowest weight I've ever achieved in adult life.

I'm determined to keep the fat content in my body as low as possible because breast cancer is linked to fat as that's where the hormones are stored.

My short term goal is to lose another 3.5 kg. Wish me luck!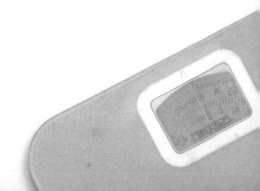

The Durian Feast

Now you've got to understand some
thing about my brother-in-law, Guna.
His understanding of a celebration is
feasting on durians. And only the very best.

As a family, we've never been crazy about
durians. In fact, Bessie finds it so repulsive she
doesn't come downstairs till we've cleared
the fruit and deodorised the dining room. Raja
and I eat durian if it's 'convenient'. We wouldn't,
for example, bother to wait in line for designer
durians or the maiden fruits of the season.

However, when I was on chemotherapy I devel-
oped a penchant for durians. My tastebuds were
as good as dead – couldn't taste a thing, and the
nerve endings in the nostrils weren't working
too well either. But durians were different from
other foods.

The durian's appeal for a chemo patient are its powerful aroma and strong-tasting pulp. The pungent or heavenly (whichever way you prefer to look at it) smell blasts through the partially functioning nerve endings in the nostrils. It banishes all thoughts of calorie control. No qualms whatsoever. The salivary glands then begin to function in anticipation of the creamy, bittersweet luscious pulp. Its taste gives you a kind of high unlike any other.

Guna gets his durians from one of the most famous durian sellers in Singapore. He's never been disappointed with the merchandise.

This is the usual ritual he carries out in preparation for the feast. He parks his car at the HDB car park a half a kilometre away, walks to the store where Mercedes', BMW's, and Lexus' are parked at its front. Guna obviously knew he wouldn't be able to find a parking lot close to the store. He makes a beeline for his usual Seller who picks the fruit for him from the $5 per fruit pile – the best doesn't necessarily have to be the most expensive.

The Seller then goes through a very complex exercise to choose the best durians for Guna. He first grasps the fruit by the stalk and scrutinises it looking for worm holes, splits or blade marks –

in case someone has slit it to take a peek inside. He then holds the fruit close to his nostrils and takes a few deep breaths. Next he shakes the durian close to his ear. A hollow rattle means there isn't too much flesh around the seed and no sound means it's probably unripe. If the fruit passes that test, he will slice away the stem to ensure that it's the prime yellow-flesh type.

Guna then tells him how many fruits he needs and whether it's for making *pengat** or for eating. The Seller puts the specified number of durians into a big brown paper bag, plus one or two extra for good measure. Guna pays for the fruits, tells him he'll see him again soon, swings the brown bag over his shoulders and walks to his car with a spring in his step. No durian load is too heavy for Guna.

This ritual has been going on for years.

So it was not surprising that Guna chose to celebrate the completion of my chemotherapy with a durian feast. We were touched by his gracious offer.

For the occasion, Guna and his son, Simon, had returned to the usual store.

* *Pengat* is a dish made with steamed white glutinous rice and deseeded durian flesh cooked in cream of coconut.

From afar, they saw the father of the durian Seller waving enthusiastically at them – he had obviously recognised Guna and Simon though he had never served them before. Business must be bad, they thought, for them to get such a warm welcome especially since they didn't own any of the fancy cars parked at the front of the store.

From afar, they looked desperately through the store for the son who normally serves them but there was no sign of him. Panic! By the time, they had arrived at the durian Seller's, Daddy-O had three durians which cost *$15 per kilo* sitting on the weighing scale. "How many people eating?" he asked. Not knowing how to tell him that they'd rather have the $5 per fruit variety, Guna meekly asked him enough for five adults and two kids, paid for them (ouch!), heaved the brown paper bag (felt somewhat heavier that day) over his shoulders and trudged back to the car.

When we arrived for the durian party, we knew nothing about the mystery-of-the-disappearing-durian-seller episode. But it was still early in the season and there's been no report of a glut so Raja and I were worried about the cost. We didn't want dear brother Guna, a minister of the Lord, to sacrifice too much for the durians.

As we discussed about the market price of durians, and how the sale of durians was affecting the Singaporean and global economy, the story slowly unfolded. We felt really bad that he had to pay so much for durians. But Guna was so happy to be celebrating the end of my chemo, he was willing to pay the exorbitant price.

How tasty can durians be that you have to pay an arm and a leg for them? We didn't think we could eat that stuff – I mean, it would probably taste metallic, like gold.

But words fail me. It was potent stuff. Intoxicating! Even with my tastebuds blunted from the chemo, I could taste the luxurious flavour. A fitting end to a painful chapter in my life.

Thanks a lot Guna, the next durian feast is on us. (But please ensure that the son is around first.)

22 Mar 1999

Hi Dr

Today is Day 3 post-Taxol. Been having a bit of a
sore throat since yesterday morning. This morning, blowing out mucus that's thick and green
and also from throat. Should I start Ciprobay?
500mg bd?

My brother-in-law brought some 'designer'
durians last night and we celebrated the end of
chemo. It was intoxicating! Savoured every bite –
must be good durians bec I could taste them in
spite of my blunted tastebuds. But I guess it
didn't help the sore throat...

So start Ciprobay?
Ciao

_____

22 Mar 1999

Ha! that's for not sharing the durians. Yes, I think
you should start the Ciprobay.

Radiation – The Breeze that Turned into a Storm

After chemotherapy was completed, I had to undergo radiotherapy. Radiotherapy consisted of 28 shots plus three boosters, a total of 31 sessions spanning six weeks. I had to go in for treatment everyday except weekends and public holidays.

Radiation, my cancer buddies told me, would be a breeze.

One said that unlike chemo, she drove herself back and forth everyday for her radiation. Another said not only did she drive herself back and forth, she actually went to work after the treatment everyday. Didn't miss a day of work. *Gee*, I thought, *if these people could do that, so can I.*

I looked forward to normal life again after chemo. Daily walks of 8 km minimum or 11 km on a good day. Regular marketing and grocery shopping trips. 'Catch-up' and 'celebration' lunches and teas with friends. I could even join the crowds in the Great Singapore Sale, since my radiation would be done in the vicinity of Orchard Road.

Unfortunately, radiation was anything but a breeze for me. In fact, it turned out to be a storm. I was tired from day one. And the tiredness got worse as the rays accumulated in my body like tons of bricks. A heavy fatigue which I'd never felt before set in. Initially I thought I was coming down with a flu but the other symptoms never came.

The scattered rays caused my stomach to feel queasy. My throat became sore and my tastebuds altered drastically. It was like having the side effects of chemotherapy permanently. At least with chemotherapy, the nausea and altered tastebuds needed only to be endured for a few days. With chemo, there was reprieve between cycles; with radiation, there was none.

The first appointment was a long one. About an hour. It was the Planning Session. I was brought to a room and I had to undress the parts that were going to be radiated – the left chest and axilla, and the left side of the back of the chest. Using a simulator and taking lots of X-rays, the technician measured and mapped out areas such as where my ribs were in relation to the heart, and so on. She marked the areas with a black marker pen. The information was then fed into a computer which calculated the precise angles at which the area of my body should be radiated.

The following day, I commenced radiation therapy.

When Bessie came with me to the radiation centre for the first time, I asked the technicians to show her around the strong room where the radiation shots were given.

The huge room was cold and daunting. Like an execution chamber. The first thing that catches the eye is the linear accelerator. This machine accelerates radioactive particles and shoots them directly at the body part they're intended for, like some high-tech laser machine.

The scene looked like it came out of a sinister sci-fi movie. I was placed on a cold, narrow black table. This table was then mechanically lifted about a metre off the floor, and moved into position. The black markings on my body had to be aligned with light indicators from the machine.

Lying beneath this intimidating machine, I often imagined that someone might key in the wrong instructions, and the arm of the machine would crush me.

The machine whirred as its well-oiled parts moved with precision, making an ominous sound in the chilly chamber.

Once I was in position, Bessie had to leave the room with the technicians. The metal door, at least a foot thick, would automatically close behind them. The room was sealed. Tight. This prevented the rays from escaping and zapping everyone else.

Then Mummy was all alone in the frigid, tightly-sealed cell, being cooked at 180 rads of radiation (a chest X-ray is a fraction of a rad).

Radiation is a very surreal experience. When my body parts have been precisely aligned with the machine, the rays are fired. This is where faith comes in. The rays are not visible nor can they be felt. But the rays are there, the technicians assured me. And they are very powerful.

For a minute or two I have to maintain my precarious position. My left hand would grip a

metal bar at the left corner of the table till it was
sore from stiffness. With my body tilted just
enough to align the markings with the light,
I worried constantly. *What if I rolled off the table
and suffer a concussion? Or worse, if some other
parts of the body were zapped by the potent rays?*

Because there is no way I could tell if the radiation had been done correctly, I worried whenever
a new technician came on duty. Everything has to
be precise – *what if she didn't do it right and the
cancer cells are not shot at but some other good
body part is?* I felt safer with the usual ones
because they were familiar with my 'case'.

Although she never said so, the radiation and
everything connected with radiation therapy must
have scared Bessie out of her wits. Maybe that's
why, after a couple of visits, she stopped coming
with me.

I knew that Bessie hated those ink markings on my
body; I had seen the disgust in her eyes whenever
she saw them when I was undressing at home.
They remind her of the agonising treatments I was
going through. And the fact that I had cancer.

The radiation treatments soon drew to a close.
Toward the end of the radiation treatment, I

resorted to parking illegally by the side entrance to the radiation department. The journey back to the nearest parking lot was too difficult to manage. This was the best solution I could find.

The last few shots were scheduled at 2 pm. I'd arrive precisely at 1.55 pm, park my nondescript nine-year-old grey Mazda 626 on the turf, hurry in for the treatment and drive off by 2.10 pm.

Finally, I completed the last dose of radiotherapy. Relieved, I hurried toward the exit door of the radiotherapy department, glad that I never have to set foot in there again. But *just* as I stepped out the door, I saw the traffic policeman zooming off on his motorcycle. He had given me a parking ticket.

I huffed at the offending pink summons pinned under the windscreen wiper, flapping cheekily in the wind. The only consolation was that I didn't have to park like this or come for radiation again.

The storm caused by radiotherapy abated with time. It took me more than six months to gradually recover my strength.

21 Sep 1999

Hi,

The last couple of weeks I was going thru a bit of depression. I'm sure menopause has sth to do with it. But I think I was going thru the grieving stage which I didn't have time for earlier on bec I was too busy getting treatment and coping with side effects and complications.

Many bks say that survivors go into depression around the time of their 1st anniversary. Raja said we should prove them wrong. Then I started to think a lot about recurrence and how I may not be here next year or how I may not be able to see Bessie graduate... and feeling sad all the time.

Last week I worked on a project with my previous company and went to Bali to cover the conference from Sat and returned yesterday evening. While there, I worked very hard and enjoyed it thoroughly. I was surprised how strong I was and I didn't feel the fatigue I'd been feeling before the trip.

It also took my mind off cancer. I came back in good spirits and upbeat. I think the break was good for me altho Raja said the job stress may not be so good for me.

Today is the 1st anniversary of my diagnosis and thank God I'm doing fine. A year on and counting! May there be many more to come.

I'm taking things easy nowadays. Just doing what I feel like doing and Not doing what I don't feel like doing. (Why wasn't I allowed to do that before??) It doesn't help that I feel so fatigued all the time and I still can't start a regular walking/exercise program.

I've started a program to lose wt. I need to get rid of the fat in my body bec oestrogen is stored in it and breast cancer is oestrogen-dependent.

Appreciate your prayers.

God bless
Grace

---

28 Sep 1999

It was good to hear from you. Indeed your one year anniversary is a significant milestone and we join you in celebrating God's gracious mercy and care!!
I was sorry to hear that you are battling depression, but I wouldn't think that would be so unusual considering all that you have been through and also considering the move to Indo. You are in the midst of a

major time of loss and transition without even considering the battle with cancer.

I will be praying for you as you get started in the weight loss program, make new friends and discover new ways to use your talents and gifts. May your joy in your relationship with the Lord be your source of comfort, strength and peace!

Elaine

Cancerous Discrimination

A month before my diagnosis, I gave up my job as Senior and Project Editor to accompany Raja on a posting to Jakarta. Ten days after our move, I found the cancerous lump and returned to Singapore for treatment.

Two weeks after my operation to remove the lump, and a week after my first cycle of chemotherapy, I was walking my usual 8 km and doing everything I was doing before my diagnosis.

My second cycle of chemotherapy confirmed what my oncologist had said – that the first cycle was indicative of the next seven. Chemo obviously didn't affect my lifestyle. Once I knew that for sure, I felt it was time to get a job.

As I flipped through the Recruitment section of the *Straits Times*, it dawned on me that no one would be willing to employ me because I have cancer.

Sure enough, each job enquiry was quickly brought to a close when I mentioned that I had cancer. Whether it was to man the telephone or to run an editorial department. Not now. Not when I finished my chemo.

I remember recruiting staff in my previous jobs. All things being equal, we would employ the candidate who didn't, say, have asthma or ventricular septal defect (VSD, commonly known as 'hole-in-the-heart'). Any medical condition that might diminish the person's productivity is an immediate barrier to his or her employability. It's a fact of life, however unfair that is.

Raja's first job offer was retracted when his medical examination revealed that he had VSD. Never mind that he never got sick and was fitter than most of his peers – he played hockey and cricket for the school, our home state of Kedah, and later, the university. What more cancer? I spelt high medical bills and weeks of paid medical leave. Even if I said I'd accept a job without any medical benefits, they'd doubt my dependability and wonder about my absenteeism. In short, I'm a liability.

Soon after my first chemo, I decided to go to the newly-opened Breast Cancer Foundation to offer my services.

"Wonderful!" said the person in charge. "How long ago did you have cancer?"

"I was diagnosed three weeks ago," I said. "I've had partial mastectomy and have just started chemo. My hair is due to fall out next week."
I thought I heard her jaw drop. But she recovered quickly and soon I was involved in an orientation meeting for those who manned their hotline.

Did it mean that I was suitable only to do volunteer work? That I could not be gainfully employed to drive a publication or two, as I used to? Believe me, it's not the money; it's the joy of doing something I love. I felt like I was serving a life sentence for having contracted cancer.

Following rejections by prospective employers, I settled into a routine of permanent vacation. I had to. I took my walks in the cool of the morning before the sun rose; kept in touch with friends by email and snail mail; lunched out every once in a while; read the books I've always wanted to read but never had time for; attended support group meetings and planned our next vacation.

In fact, I dreamed up a few exotic expeditions for the family. I'm still dying (it's not a forbidden word in our family) to do that one-day walk on the Tongariro Crossing on North Island. Then there's Serengeti or Kruger. For some reason (which Raja and Bessie are not telling me) we always end up going somewhere not as wild or as exciting. Interlaken in Switzerland last year wasn't too bad actually...

I've since settled comfortably into freelance writing. Funny how the editors of the publications trust me to deliver the goods for every issue but they would not employ me full-time.

Still, I'm thankful for the mercy of work. I throw myself into it and I often have to be wrenched away from the computer. It's fun, it's therapeutic and it keeps me sane.

But however exciting the assignments are, freelance writing will never be as fulfilling as managing a publication. How I miss the din of the editorial department. The deadlines that drive me crazy. The satisfaction of putting another issue to bed.

Bessie's Story

B essie had the privilege to apply to the National Honor Society (NHS) of the Jakarta International School (JIS) where she was to be a senior the following year. This was one of four essays she wrote for the application.

* * *

Looking back over your life, has anything special happened to you that sets you apart and makes you different from other students?

* * *

My mother was diagnosed with breast cancer in 1998. We had just moved to Jakarta at the time and I had just started school at the British International School (BIS). My mother and my father had to move back to Singapore for a year so that my mother could undergo treatment and in the meanwhile, I stayed on at BIS so that I could complete my GCSE exams. I tried to fly down to Singapore at least once a month.

The experience of having to live apart from my parents while my mother was very ill in Singapore was heart wrenching. I was worried for my mother and her health, and my parents on their side, were worried about me. However, as painful as the whole situation was, it taught me many things.

First of all, it taught me the value of life. Until then, I had never expected anything of such magnitude to happen to one so close to me. Cancer always seems to happen to 'somebody else'. When it happened, I began to see that life is fragile, and the relationships that we have with people are precious. My relationship with my mother certainly deepened when I realised that I might not have her for much longer. My relationship with my father grew stronger too, as we had to be strong together for my mother.

The experience made me re-evaluate my priorities. Till then, school and achieving academically was my utmost priority. I suppose I connected success in school to success in life. But when my mother fell ill, all my other priorities dimmed in the light of my relationship with my mother. I realised that there will be lots of opportunities to achieve in life, but the relationships one has with people are fleeting.

I really treasure my family now.

Living away from my parents taught me how to be emotionally independent. Until I was 15, I was incredibly close to my parents. And while I value their views and their support in my life now, I feel like I am not completely dependent on them. I suppose that detachment from them was part of the process of growing up. But it was accelerated in my case because of my physical detachment from them. Now my parents and I have achieved the 'friends' status in our relationship and we all like it this way.

Finally, I have become more aware of cancer now that I know I have a risk of developing it. I have become a vegetarian, as doctors say animal fats are carcinogenic. Moreover, I know how to help other cancer-stricken families. Support among the 'cancer community' is very important and I try to help those that I know.

My mother has gone through chemotherapy and her body is still slowly recovering from it's devastating effects. However, she is up and about and lives a very full life. She has taught me how to be strong. I know that every day I have with her is a gift from God and I will make the most of it for it may be all I have.

Hello, I Read Your Article

Inspired by my being bald and the funny ways people responded to it, I wrote an article and sent it to the *Straits Times' Life!* section. A couple of weeks later, I wrote another article about the frustration of not being able to get a job because of cancer.

Two more articles were published in quick succession a couple of months later under the *Viewpoint* column of the *Straits Times*. This spurred me on to write even more as I went through the stages of treatment and as I sorted out my own emotions. But what thrilled me most were the responses from readers. I was amazed that people *actually read* my articles, and that they bothered to contact me.

When we moved to Jakarta a year later, I continued to write for *Life!* and also started writing for the *Jakarta Post*.

Thus began the exciting relationships with my readers. I responded to every one who had called the *Straits Times* about my articles, and to every email I received. I have since met many of these readers, and kept in touch with the others by phone or through email.

Some readers have been touched by cancer – through knowing someone who had cancer or through having contracted it themselves. But many were attracted simply because these articles candidly spoke, not merely about cancer, but about life.

They cared enough to contact me. I was encouraged and touched by their messages and calls.

Here are some of these messages. They are reproduced here with the writers' permission.

---

3 Feb 2000

Hello,
I wrote to say that I enjoyed reading your articles – your frustration at not getting employment after your diagnosis, your making friends with a lady who also sought treatment at Marine Parade polyclinic and your patronage at some eating place at Upper East Coast Road.

I was impressed by your cheerfulness so I set down to write to you in 1998 after I read your articles, hoping to bring you some cheer. Then I underwent surgery and was diagnosed with kidney cancer in July 1999.

I thought of you and I became very positive about the whole thing. Being positive did help me and all those near and dear to me. I must thank you for helping me indirectly through your articles. You may not realise how your articles touch others.

I am fine now. When I returned to the office after my leave, I found the letter that I wrote but I destroyed it (regret doing it now) because I thought it was of no use to anyone. You had not written for some time. So I was very glad to see your article and your email address in the papers this morning. So here I am writing to you. I hope you are very much better and I hope this letter will bring you some cheer.

Warmest regards
Betty Nah

4 Feb 2000

hello ms grace...
i read ur article 'Dealing With Illness' in the ST, Life,
on 3/2/2000 (thursdae) and i truly understand wat u
mean abt not knowing wat to say to a person who is
ill. this is bcos i have a very close gal fren whose sis
is very seriously ill due to a very rare type of cancer.
this had certainly been a terrible blow to my fren n
her family. being her close fren, it realli saddens us
to see dat she is trying to put up a strong front even
though she is actually struggling wif the pain &
sadness deep down inside everydae.

but, we realli dunno wat to do to make her or her sis feel
better cos we ain't God or doctors! we din dare to bring
up the matter in front of her. Furthermore, she did tell
us dat she dun wanna tok abt it so we respect her. on
the other hand, we juz dun feel so right cos itz like we
aren't concern abt her when we dun ask anything... u
noé wat i mean??? so we are pretty trapped!

anyway, frm ur article, ur methods are mostly
directed at the ill person herself/himself... den wat
abt the ill person's family?? wat can we do to make
them feel better???... hope dat u can advise... sorrie
abt the abruptness of my mail... thanx for reading...
regards... Leigh

*(Author's note: Donch u jus lurve the way Leigh rites? Her email always
cheers me up.)*

88

3 Feb 2000

Ms Grace,
I first read your sharings in *Life!* (*Straits Times*) last year.
I've been wanting to write to you, but I did not know
how. Today's article must be His plan for us to get
acquainted – finally.

I just want to say, i think it is very brave of you to fight
cancer. It must be horrible to be going through chemo,
which I've often read abt and saw in the movies. Losing
an important part of you – your breasts – must be another
big blow too.

I am still young and very much protected in this country.
So I do not know what "hardship" /"resilience" / "kindness" really mean. Most of the time, I am just preoccupied with trying to pass my exams.

Your sharings have reminded me to look beyond all that.
Thank you so much.

I pray that you are fully healed too. Let's stay in touch.
You make a good friend to keep.

Shalom
Gwen Sin

3 Feb 2000

Hi Grace!
Remember me. I'm Marianne Pereira, one of your
breast cancer *"kakis"* who contacted you after your
features in the Life section of ST. Just to let you know
that " I too am still alive!!!" Remembered you once
more when I read your "Hello, you still alive?" today.

Take care, I am doing fine, taking Tamoxifen, have
decided to keep my hair short and am generally happy
as I am back at work.

All the best and do email me when you can find the
time.

By the way
Marianne Pereira

2 Jan 2000

Have just read your article in the *Jakarta Post* this
morning.

What really triggered this email was that my wife also
picked up the 'short straw' and reading your article
reminded me of so many words, thoughts, aspirations
etc that we lived through. She was diagnosed with
breast cancer on 1 Apr 96; had a mastectomy on 26 Apr

96 and was given two years to live on 16 May 96. She
finally passed away on 14 Jan 99 and so the first anniversary of her death is 12 days away.

She was 50 at the time of her death and whilst still young
had packed a lot into those 50 years. Not only was she a
mother of our two sons but she lived life to the max (apart
from the final two difficult years). She was a shopoholic
and her cv listed that she had a 'black belt in shopping'.

However, what I wanted to share with you were just a
couple of thoughts. Having said that and naturally
having read your article, I am convinced that you are
on the right track. The buzz words you use are good
positives! All you have to do is abide by them!!!!!

Perhaps you should not forget that whilst you have this
cancer, those around you — your family and friends —
are also suffering — perhaps in a 'funny' way more than
you. As I have always said 'A problem shared is a
problem halved'. Try and be honest with those around
you. If you don't feel well then tell them — perhaps tell
them to get out of your space whilst you are having a
downer, but try not to hold too much from them
because they will pick up the vibes that all is not right
and will be eager to help if only you give them the ok.
So, help those around you!

I enjoyed your story about the photographs. We followed the same process and the hundreds of photo-

graphs are now a lasting memory of such a dear woman. Of course some were not all 'happy' photographs but they all formed a tapestry of her and our life. On her death – a death that I wanted to happen so that she was rid of her suffering – we celebrated her life rather than mourned her death.

I wish you all the very very best. You sound a very positive person – stay positive. Have a ball – live life to the max but don't be too proud to share your life with those around you. All the very best to you – and your family.

Kia ora
Raymond J. Seymour

[Author's note: Raja and I met up with Raymond for dinner and we learnt so much from his experience. He is now fishing in North island, NZ.]

Cancer Buddies

I opened my email this morning and got this message from a friend:

Molly Chacko passed away in KL last Sat 22 April 2000 at 8:30pm, funeral the next day. She died peacefully.

Auntie Molly was in her 60's and a member of our church. She had recurrent breast cancer ten years after her first diagnosis. Instead of saying, "Why me, again?" or complaining about the agonising treatment that she was going to undergo soon, I remember her telling me: "I'm thankful that God gave me a bonus of ten years."

I was diagnosed with cancer shortly afterwards. We underwent chemo the same time – she did hers in Kuala Lumpur (she was a Malaysian) while I did mine in Singapore.

Sharon Matthew, her daughter who lives in Singapore, kept us abreast of her progress. Auntie Molly and I wrote each other cards and letters.

I remember her visit to Singapore last year. I saw her sitting on the pew on the other side of the aisle looking radiant with her new crop of completely white hair.

After the service, we just hugged each other, remembering silently the ordeal we'd just gone through and thanking God for life. We exchanged important details like the exact dates when I took off my hat and when she took off her wig. Our hair was still very short and close to the scalp. We both looked very trendy because crew cut was in vogue then.

She had just sent us an Easter card. In it she told us about how she was going for a review on 24 April to see if the radiation had stopped the spread of cancer on her ribs. Though she must have been in great pain, she wrote: "I am trusting in the Lord to keep me comfortable." We didn't realise how ill she was then. Only her joyful spirit shone through those words. She died the day before Easter on 22 April.

I wept when I read the email message. I shall miss Auntie Molly dearly. She was an inspiration and an encouragement.

I thank God for releasing her from pain, and for giving her a full and joyful life. Her death is an event to celebrate, for the Easter message is that she has gone to be with God in glory. And we shall surely meet again.

When I was diagnosed with cancer, many friends brought 'friends who had breast cancer' to encourage us. We began to make friends with breast cancer survivors as well as survivors of other cancers. I call them my 'cancer buddies'. We were surprised how common the disease was. I guess we never noticed the numbers before because there was no reason to do so.

It's amazing how quickly people with cancer bond. The tie that binds is the deadly disease. In woundedness and pain, cancer buddies and their families tend to open their hearts to each other. They receive comfort and they give comfort in return.

My cancer buddies were people who understood the depths of what I was experiencing. And I them. We were kindred spirits on this journey through life-threatening illness. A journey that led us through pain and into strange, new lands that were not of our own choosing.

When two women with breast cancer meet, they tend to compare notes.

When were you diagnosed? What stage was it? How many lymph nodes were positive?
Who was your surgeon?
What did s/he do – lumpect or mastect? How's your arm? Any lymphadema? Mine's still stiff, got to work on it more.
Who's your oncologist? Is s/he nice? Can you talk to him or her? I'm on eight cycles of ACT, what are you on? I've finished three cycles, what about you? Did you join any support group? I'm sorry to hear you have a recurrence. How did you find out? How bad is it? Do you have to go for chemo?

Cancer buddies are usually at different stages of the illness. It's nice to meet someone who's at the same stage as you – just a couple of weeks before or after you in a similar treatment. You compare every minute detail that is happening in your lives. And you are relieved to find out that your enormous appetite, infections and emotional highs immediately after chemo (due to the steroids given as premedication) are normal phenomena after all.

It's also wonderful to meet someone healthy and normal-looking, who has been through it six months or a year ago. You look at the person and hope to see yourself looking just as well six months or a year on. You are filled with hope. You are encouraged to persevere and trudge through the remaining cycles of chemo. Suddenly the road doesn't seem so long or the burden as heavy.

Sometimes you meet someone who's had a recurrence or is dying from breast cancer. You pray for her healing. You pray that God will hold her in His arms and comfort her and her family as they deal with death. You pray that it will not happen to you. Not just yet, anyway.

Isn't it ironic that the cancer, which brought us together and sealed our friendship, is the same thing that causes us to part in death?

It's a bittersweet experience. But I've been inspired by the courage, the strength, the grace, the transparency and the peace that prevails in the lives of my cancer buddies.

The comfort that I received when I had cancer, I now want to share with others who are going through cancer. Especially breast cancer.

Mar 2000

My experience with breast cancer is helping mastectomy patients fit their prosthesis for the first time.
I would accompany a down and unsmiling lady into
the small changing room, help them position the
prosthesis in their bra and then watch their faces light
up like a little girl receiving a treasured gift. Never
did I have to wrap the product up because they'll be
wearing it out of the shop and leaving with an empty
box. Transformed. A woman again. I have never
refused a chance to serve such a customer. The most
rewarding of sales experiences ever.

Sook Mei

---

14 Oct 1998

I think it is a jolly good idea to take control and shave
your hair. Then you don't wait for things to happen – you
know when it will happen and you had planned for it.

I didn't always wear a wig. I had a natural look at
home – my family loved me, whether I was bald or not.
Outside the home, I used the scarf a lot, and friends
and acquaintances who did not know me well, thought
I was fashionable. The scarf was cooler (temperature-
wise) than the wig. On cooler days, or occasions when

I knew I should wear a wig, I did. So there are choices.

I have a full head of hair now, I wish it wouldn't grey, but it does and I'm thankful for my full head.

Do look forward to your last chemo when the hair starts growing. I donned the 'Twiggy' look, and again the world thought I was 'cool'! (and brave) of course. I had lost some weight then, and did look quite well, lah!

Capitalise on your new look, baby! And you CAN look good, alright? Dress well and look well. I had a few new things to go with the new scarves and you can even have long and short hair wigs.

Talk to me about the practical things like hair and thirst, if they are bothersome to you, Grace. They are not trivial at all. I will tell you my experiences but I do not want to pre-empt your experiences, because the doctors had always said that each one's experiences are different.

Meanwhile, be happy, thankful for medical advancement, and pray. God bless.

Love
Elizabeth

16 Oct 1998

Not the religious scarves, darling...I mean the fashionable European ones. Metro or Takashimaya or similar
departmental stores have them. Don't tie the scarves like
a 'samsui' woman – you know, like construction women
workers with the red headgear. I think generally, don't
knot it under your chin, but tie it behind your neck. The
style that is really 'hip' is the pirate-style – looks really
great when you wear a pantsuit.

You'll be okay, baby. Look fashionable.

You need to let go, things aren't as important as they
seem. This week I learnt the lesson again that the world
turns round no matter what.

Nice talking to you. Yes, let's have a meal. When Raja needs
to go away, do give me a call – we girls can go gallivanting. I'm always game to go makan and jalan jalan.

Love, Elizabeth

15 Jun 1999

Dearest Grace,
I am sorry to hear that you went though such a tough
period. You probably have no idea how important and
encouraging your kind words, articles and cards were

when I was experiencing a tough time. Thank you very very much for everything and I apologise for not having been able to do the same for you.

In life and especially in difficult times it is good to have role models who inspire positive thinking. You surely are one. I hope the worst is now over for you and that things are getting better.

Just over two weeks ago, I had my last chemo and lumbar punctures (one of them by an inexperienced doctor!). The MRI didn't show any trace of tumor and my doc said that I was clear of cancer cells. Time to open the champagne bottle.

I have started working again, because for me that is one of the best cures. I had an infection of the airways recently. Though the infection is not completely gone, I feel stronger by the day. The future looks bright. No more poking needles, no more medicines etc. Only my hair is refusing to grow.

I hope some good old normality will also return to your life. Speedy recovery and let's stay in touch.

Sayonara
Ernesto Braam
(Tokyo)

Healing Words

66You've got mail."

I was so hooked on email, I'd sometimes bring
my notebook to the hospital when I was admitted
so I could update friends and receive encouragement from them. When the notebook wasn't
available, my family would print the messages
from home and do my correspondence by proxy.

After days of high fever when both body and spirit
were spent, I remember how encouraging it was to
receive email that said: "Hang in there". It gave
me the heart to plod on because someone cared.
Or my oncologist would send a simple email:
"Haven't heard from you for a while. How are
you?" In his wilder moments he'd write, "Hello.
You still alive?"

Besides email there were e-cards, cards that came
with flowers, and snail mail. These all meant so

much to me. Someone sent me a tape in the mail twice. It meant I was thought of. Made me feel better right away. And there were other lifelines...

"I brought you flowers." This is a time-tested gesture, and I can affirm that it works. What is it about flowers that cheers an ailing person's heart? Is it the colour, the type of flower, the fresh fragrance, or the fragile, tender petals? I'm not sure what it is exactly but I do know that flowers have a way of cheering me up. Whether it's a single stalk or an exuberant bouquet. I prefer them simply wrapped in paper and unarranged because I then have the pleasure of arranging them myself. That is therapy.

I remember how a bouquet of flowers came to my aid soon after my last round of chemo. That weekend, I found a lump on the other breast. The days slunk by, long and dark, as we waited for the Tuesday appointment with my oncologist. After a full morning of harrowing investigations, I came home and found two dozen red roses and baby's breath waiting for me. I felt so loved. Our friends had read our hearts correctly and sent the flowers. I sunk my face deep into the cool velvet petals and drank in their fragrant balm.

A hug and "Take care." Words fail when we
don't know what turn the disease will take.
Even now I don't quite know what to say to
friends who have just been diagnosed with cancer.

Immediately after my diagnosis when I was
devastated, and whenever I fell ill, it meant a lot
when friends gave me a hug or put their arm
round my shoulders and said, "Take care." They
did not dish out preachy or glib words like "God
will heal you", nor did they give careless silence.
The simple touch meant they cared, whether I got
better or not. That was comfort for me.

"Thought you might like to read this book."
Friends brought books on just about anything –
jokes, novels, cancer, healing, nutritional therapy.
The books were indeed welcome. Not that I read
them all (I will, one day). But they were gifts
of love.

Initially, we wanted to read everything on cancer
so books on cancer and its treatment came in
handy. Later on, the other books helped me to
pass time and to reflect on issues such as healing,
and life and death.

"I'm praying for you." During illness, especially
one that's life threatening, prayer gives hope. I find

strength in knowing that someone is praying for me. For really, at the end of the day, my life is not in my hands. But I can plead, and my friends can plead for me, for health and long life.

"Wanna do lunch?" As I got stronger and began to pick up my routine after each bout of illness, I was always thrilled to get a call or email that asked me to lunch. Friends who are in tune with your condition will know when exactly to ask.

Going to lunch with a friend gives me an opportunity to do something different. Life gets pretty predictable and boring when you are sick. You're at home all the time and the most exciting thing you do is wait for the postman or check your email every hour.

It also gives me an opportunity to talk to someone else other than my helper. Doing lunch with a friend was filled with as much anticipation as preparing for a safari trip in Africa!

I used to be tongue-tied when I was around friends who were ill. Now having received and learnt, I think I'm a better giver, a better comforter and supporter.

Looking back, especially over the periods when I was ill from infections and operations, I see the simple things that friends did or said which lighted up my life like shafts of brightness piercing through darkness.

As Asians, we often avoid talking about some things. Feelings. Fears. Expressions of love. But we need to. It is not weak, nor is it 'western'. To love and to be loved are basic human needs.

So go ahead. Show your love. And say it well.

Seize the Day!

Ten weeks after my last chemo, I was glad to take off the hat and proudly display my new crop of hair. It was luxurious and full. There were both the black *and* the grey. The oncologist had promised me that the hair will surely return but he didn't tell me that greys were coming back as well!

Two weeks later I went to Helen, my hairdresser, to tidy up the straggly bits around the ears. That was my first haircut in months. Helen was so pleased to see me (and to see me so well) that she didn't charge for the job.

Raja had stopped playing cricket on weekends since I started treatment. He wanted to be around in case I fell sick. Then one day after treatment had ended, he called me from the office and said that his company's team was short of players in a league game. I said, "Go for it." So he started playing cricket again on weekends. It was like pre-cancer days.

I soon found myself falling into a routine that didn't include trips to the hospital. No more doctors fussing over me. No chemo every 21 days, no more gruelling trips to the radiation department. Now I had time to read, write and shop. I indulged in leisurely morning strolls because I was under no pressure to keep another doctor's appointment.

I had no difficulty rolling right back into routines. I didn't miss the adrenaline-charged highs that followed each cycle of treatment. I didn't experi-ence the anti-climax many cancer patients feel when treatment ended and medical attention was withdrawn.

I began to hear from people a lot less. I didn't get the dialogue box on my computer that said 'Retrieving 17 messages' each time I checked for email. In fact I was lucky if I got any mail at all. Phone calls dropped to a normal level.

My daughter moaned that nobody loved us any more because we didn't hear from people as often. Much as I like to receive mail, I was not unhappy about it because it meant that I was getting back on my feet.

The days of social inertia came to an end. Three weeks after my treatment ended, I went out for an evening formal for the first time since I was diagnosed.

Raja had been keeping formal engagements on his own because I never knew how I was going to be feeling, and so did not accept any invitations. Now it was nice to have occasion to dress up again.

The crisis was over; 'normal' life had begun. We'd come full circle, it was business as usual. The ephemeral had dissipated and normalcy had returned.

When I mentioned to Raja how the cancer seemed just a bad dream, his pained response was, "Not for me it wasn't. It was *real.*"

I had been so busy fighting all this while, I didn't have time to think about what life could be without cancer. Now that treatment was over and I entered the world of wellness again, the cancer-ridden days seemed so distant.

But niggling thoughts persisted: is it really business as usual? And what is normalcy for me?

Finally, I came to realise that I was *not* like everyone else. *I am different*. I had cancer and I could have cancer again.

I live on the edge. Whenever something is amiss – when there's pain in my bones or when I feel a lump – I think cancer has returned. Call it paranoia if you like but I think no cancer survivor should ignore these signs and symptoms. Early detection saves lives.

Yet, hope springs eternal – never has the adage been more true. I've learned that statistics and the median doesn't have to mean *me*.

I've adopted a defiance about the disease – it may or may not recur but I won't lead a smaller life because of it. Because of cancer, I live a fuller life. Life to the max.

Before I had cancer, I lived like I had all the time in the world; three score and ten years seemed an eternity. But after coming so close to losing my life, I seize each moment, each day with an urgency, as if I'm going to lose it tomorrow.

I make the most of my life. I take risks. I'm not off to scale Mt Everest – but then again I might. Friends know I enjoy a challenge. I say "yes" to a great many things – after all, what have I got to lose? But I also say "no" to a lot things in order to say "yes" to the things worth giving my time to.

I live this fragile life without fear because I know God holds my hand and He holds my future. In the seminary of the cancer ward, I learned over and over again that God is faithful and He is good. He is here for me. Always.

* * *

One of my favourite things is to watch the sun set from a window seat on a plane. Sunset is always glorious up there above the clouds; the rays are magnificent, the colours ever changing. It feels so much closer to heaven there at dusk than anywhere else on earth.

Each time that I watched the sun set, I imagined that when it's time for me to die I shall soar majestically into the sunset.

After this dance with cancer, death has become real. And sunsets above the clouds have become more poignant.

But until it is time for my spirit to soar into the sunset, I sojourn on, not yielding a second of exuberant life to the fear of death.

Cheers to life!

The interregnum came to an end quickly. It was time to move on. We continued the disrupted chapter where we left off, as I resumed my posting to Jakarta, bringing Grace along, to be reunited with Bessie after that long period of being apart.

The posting in Jakarta brought new challenges for me, as we came at a time when tumultuous events were unleashing themselves upon the country. There were new staff to work with, new contacts to be made, a new marketplace to tackle. It was exhilarating in a strange way, as though I had been in suspended animation, in a pupa stage, for three-quarters of a year, and had now emerged to my original calling. Not that the previous nine months had been inactive months; professionally I grew a lot in the place I served. But it was nice to be overseas again.

Bessie is on her last lap before she goes off to university. She has had a wonderful year, with the family with her, with new friends, a great school, and the challenges that a liberal education brings. She has done well academically, but more important, she is discovering herself, realising that she can do almost anything if she sets her mind to it. The year of trial has lit a fire in her belly. Nothing so pleases a parent as to see the child grow in grace and truth, balanced in all aspects of life.

Grace has been having a more difficult time than the two of us. The stresses and strains of the change, plus the environment in Jakarta causes her allergies to act up ever so frequently. Her auto immune system must somehow have been affected with all the treatment she had to endure. But medical checks with her doctors in Singapore every two months have shown her to be free of cancer. We have much to give thanks for.

On the whole we have managed. We count our blessings with every passing day. We continue to live one day at a time. Every visit to the doctor we pray for continued healing. We are thankful we have come through the crisis. Not unscathed, but safe. And, we hope, stronger. Ready to face the next trial, and ready to help others who are going through their valley.

We are thankful for the blessings of failure, for they have kept us human and humble. There are now things we can empathise with in others that we would not even have remotely identified with before. The blessing of pain has caused us to grow, for only the pruned shrub brings forth much fruit. And we have enjoyed the blessing of hope, knowing that the God who has brought us safe thus far will surely bring us safely home.

I need to convey a personal note of thanks to the many friends and their family members who have rallied around during our moment of need. There are too many to mention, but they would know who they are. They came not asking to be recognised, only to give and to love. It has been a privilege to have walked through the valley of the shadow of death with God, but also in your company. For you all have held our hands, lit a light to brighten the dark paths, and helped to lighten our loads.

It is a short life, this. Full of twists and turns. But at every bend there is always something to rejoice about, something to celebrate. *Carpe diem*. Seize the day. It's the only day, and the only life, you will have.

Raja Segran

GOOD BYE!